MW01128317

Molly Morningstar
A Doll for Me

Written by
Andrea Coke

Illustrated by
M. Fernanda Orozco

Front cover image by M. Fernanda Orozco
Book design by Praise Saflor
Printed in Canada.
First printing edition 2021.

Toronto, ON, Canada
www.abcbooknook.com
Adventures In Reverie Publishing Corp.

Publisher's Cataloging-in-Publication data

Names: Coke, Andrea, author. | Orozco, M. Fernanda, illustrator.
Title: Molly Morningstar : a doll for me / written by Andrea Coke ; illustrated by M. Fernanda Orozco. Series: Molly Morningstar
Description: Toronto, ON: Adventures in Reverie Publishing Corp., 2021. | Summary: Molly Morningstar searches high and low for the perfect doll.
With Mama fast asleep and her dog Boomer at her side, ever-so-spunky Molly Morningstar gets creative and tackles the problem herself!
Identifiers: ISBN: 978-1-7773883-2-4 (hardcover) | 978-1-7773883-5-5 (paperback) | 978-1-7773883-1-7 (ebook)
Subjects: LCSH Girls--Juvenile fiction. | Blacks--Juvenile fiction. | African American girls--Juvenile fiction. | Dolls--Juvenile fiction. | Toys--
Juvenile fiction. | CYAC Girls--Fiction. | Blacks--Fiction. | African American girls--Fiction. | Dolls--Fiction. | Toys--Fiction. | BISAC JUVENILE
FICTION / Diversity & Multicultural | JUVENILE FICTION / Toys, Dolls & Puppets
Classification: LCC PZ7.1.C64255 Mo 2021 | DDC [E]--dc23

To the child in all of us who just wants to feel seen.

Molly peeks over her mama's shoulder.
"Hurry Mama! What does it say?"

"I will read it to you," says Mama.

>.To.: Molly Morningstar.<

It's my Birthday!!

I'm having a tea party.
I hope you can come.

My mom's baking a CAKE
and you can have some.

Bring your favorite doll
for a really great time
as a super special
guest of mine.

Love, Emma

"Yippee! I love going to Emma's house,"
shouts Molly. "She has lots of toys."

Molly runs to her room. "Come on, Boomer.
Help me choose my best doll."

Molly looks around for a special doll
to take to the party.

She looks on her shelf.

She looks in her toy box.

She even looks under her bed.

Boomer helps by nudging a doll with his nose.
"How about this one?" he seems to say.

"You sure have made a mess!" Mama says. "Which doll have you chosen?"

"I don't want to take any of these dolls to the party," moans Molly.

Molly looks at herself in the mirror.

"Emma has lots of pretty dolls. And they all look like her.
I wish I had a doll that looks like ME!"

Molly and her mom go shopping for a new doll.

The nice lady in the store says, "This is our number one best doll."

Molly looks at the doll.
She looks at a long row of dolls on
the shelf. She shakes her head.

"No. These dolls all look the same."

Molly and her mama look online.

"Nope, nothing here," says Mama.
"Just take what you have.
It's just a doll. It's not a big deal."

Molly feels sad.

At breakfast, Molly only eats half of her pancakes.
She doesn't touch her chocolate milk.
Her papa asks,

"What's wrong,
Molly Morningstar?"

"I can't find the right doll to take to the party. My dolls look like Emma, not me."

Papa says, "Don't worry, kiddo. Maybe one day we will find a doll that looks like you."

"I know what I'll do!" shouts Molly. I'll make my own doll!"

"But you don't know how to make a doll," says Mama.

"You'll see," Molly answers quietly.

While Mama takes a nap,
Molly is eager to get started.

"Let's see,"
Molly says to Boomer.
"Where shall we begin?"

The drawer pops open and everything tumbles out!

"Look, it's your favorite sock!" says Molly.
Boomer wags his tail.

"And Mama's earring!
And candy!"

Boomer helps Molly haul their treasures to the playroom.

He watches as Molly bends ...

and cuts...

and glues...

and stuffs ...

and paints.

"Hmm," says Molly, looking in the mirror.
"Now she needs hair."

Boomer yelps, then leaps out of the room.
Molly runs after him.

Perfect!

Mama's knitting yarn!

Perfect!

Molly and Boomer carry away heaping piles of yarn.

THUMP!

A big spool of shimmery brown yarn topples to the floor.

"Molly! What a mess!" says Mama.

"Sorry Mama, but look at my doll.
She looks just like me!"

While Molly cleans up the mess, she holds her new doll in her arms and softly sings:

We're going to a party, how exciting this will be!
We are perfect twins, I'm sure that you can see!
We will go together, to have a joyous day,
Feeling oh, so grateful as we love and laugh and play."

After dinner, Molly puts the final touches on her doll.
"Ta-da!"

"This doll is lucky to have you, kiddo," says Papa.

The day of the party,
Molly eats all of her pancakes.

She finishes her chocolate milk.

She tidies her room without being told.

Boomer skips along with Molly on the way to Emma's house.

"Happy birthday, Emma!"
Molly says cheerfully.

"Let's have some tea," says Emma.

"Your doll looks just like you," Emma says.

Molly is so proud. "I made her!"

"Ruff, Ruff," adds Boomer.

Molly laughs. "That means he helped, too."

Everyone loves Molly's new doll.

"I love her hair," says Farha.

"You match," says Sam.

"Can I hold her?" asks Wei.

"Look at mine!" says Teddy.

The friends take turns pouring tea.

They munch the cookies and gobble the cake.

They sing happy birthday.

They squeal when Emma opens her gifts,
and gets... another new doll!

Molly wishes she could stay longer, but the party is over.

"My friends love my doll," she tells Mama.

"Your doll is perfect, Molly Morningstar.
She's one of a kind—just like you."

Draw your own perfect doll.

Educator by day, children's author by night! Andrea Coke is known for creating engaging, diverse stories that help all kids to communicate for connection. Driven by the belief that children need to see themselves reflected in books and toys, Andrea is on a mission to bring the knowledge that ALL children matter and deserve representation, one book at a time. Proud Canadian mom of four, Andrea is originally from the twin islands of Trinidad and Tobago.

Molly Morningstar, A Doll for Me is her debut picture book.

M. Fernanda is an illustrator and graphic designer from Guatemala, based in Spain, that enjoys translating messages, ideas, even worlds into dynamic illustrations.

She has loved books since she was a little girl and was always reading. That's probably the reason why she is always excited to be part of projects involving children's literature and drawings that will give new readers a wonderful experience while reading.

Celebrate the beauty in differences.

Andrea Coke

CPSIA information can be obtained
at www.ICGtesting.com
Printed in the USA
LVHW071924080522
718198LV00014BA/529